We Can Help the Environment

Rebecca Rissman

Heinemann Library
Chicago, Illinois

www.heinemannraintree.com
Visit our website to find out more information about Heinemann-Raintree books.

To order:
☎ Phone 888-454-2279
💻 Visit www.heinemannraintree.com to browse our catalog and order online.

Edited by Rebecca Rissman, Siân Smith, and Charlotte Guillain
Designed by Kimberly Miracle and Joanna Malivoire
Picture research by Elizabeth Alexander
Originated by Heinemann Library
Printed in China by Leo Paper Group

13 12 11 10 09
10 9 8 7 6 5 4 3 2 1

Library of Congress Cataloging-in-Publication Data
Rissman, Rebecca.
   We can help the environment / Rebecca Rissman.
      p. cm.
   Includes bibliographical references and index.
   ISBN 978-1-4329-2276-4 (hc) -- ISBN 978-1-4329-2283-2 (pb) 1. Environmentalism--Juvenile literature. I. Title.
   GE195.5.R57 2008
   363.7'0525--dc22
                                            2008054583

Acknowledgments
The author and publishers are grateful to the following for permission to reproduce copyright material: Alamy pp. **7 left**, **21** (© Jim West), **11 left** (© Lourens Smak), **11 right** (© Ange), **13 right** (© Stefan Kiefer / vario images), **16 left** (© Paul Glendell), **18** (G Wolfgang Pölzer); © Capstone Global Library Ltd pp. **9 left**, **9 right**, **22 middle** (Tudor Photography); Corbis p.**8** (© LWA/Dann Tardif/Blend Images); Getty Images pp.**4** (Taxi/ Eightfish), **6** (Stone/ Ben Osborne), **16 right** (Stone/ Victoria Snowber), **17 right** (Taxi /Gary Buss); iStockphoto pp.**7 middle right** (© Ints Tomsons), **12 left** (© Hans F. Meier), **12 right** (© Jon Schulte); NaturePL.com p.**19** (Aflo); Photolibrary pp.**5** (Mark Henley/Imagestate), **10** (Dev Carr/ Cultura), **13 left** (Jeffrey Hamilton/ Stockbyte), **14** (Corbis), **15** (Creatas /Comstock), **20** (Momatiuk - Eastcott/ Flirt Collection); Shutterstock **17 left** (© newphotoservice), **22 left** (© Morgan Lane Photography), **22 right** (© newphotoservice), **7 middle left** (© Morgan Lane Photography), **7 right** (© Feng Yu).

Cover photograph of children picking up litter reproduced with permission of Corbis/ © Leland Bobbé. Back cover photograph reproduced with permission of Photolibrary (Dev Carr/Cultura).

We would like to thank Nancy Harris and Adriana Scalise for their help in the preparation of this book.

Every effort has been made to contact copyright holders of any material reproduced in this book. Any omissions will be rectified in subsequent printings if notice is given to the publisher.

Some words are shown in bold, **like this**. They are explained in "Words to Know" on page 23.

Contents

About this series

Books in this series introduce children to different ways they can help the environment. Use this book to stimulate discussion about what the environment is, how it is harmed, and how children can care for it.

What Is the Environment?

The **environment** is the world around us.

People can hurt the environment in many ways.
We need to care for the environment.

Caring for the Environment

There are many ways to care for the **environment**.

You can do something to help the environment every day.

Reusing

You can **reuse** old things instead of throwing them away. When you use an old tire to make a swing you are reusing it.

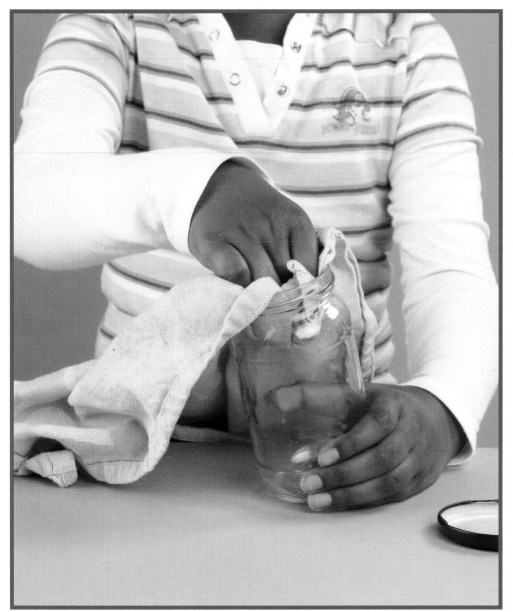 

You can reuse old jars and boxes to hold your things.
When you reuse things, you help the **environment**.

Recycling

You can **recycle**. Recycling turns old things into new things.

old paper

100% RECYCLED

new paper

You can recycle glass, metal, plastic, and paper.
When you recycle your things, you help the **environment**.

Saving Energy

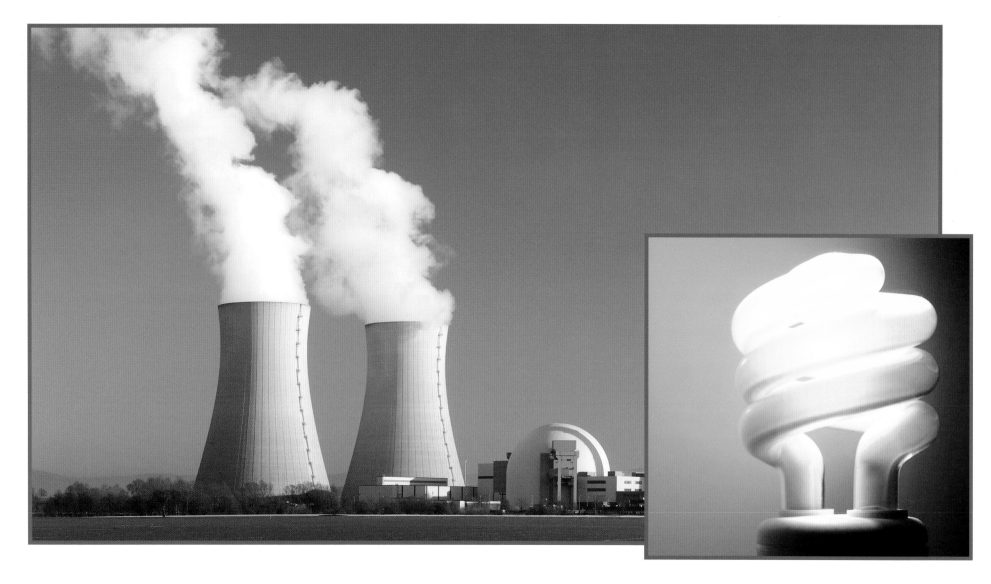

You can save **energy**. Energy makes many things work.

Lights use energy. When you turn off the lights, you save energy. **Air conditioners** use energy. When you open the window, you save energy.

Cleaning Up Litter

You can clean up litter. Litter is trash that people have dropped on the ground. Never drop litter on the ground.

Litter is bad for the **environment**. When you clean up litter, you help the environment.

Saving Water

You can save water. Taking baths uses a lot of water. Leaving the tap running uses a lot of water.

When you take a shower instead of a bath, you help the **environment**. When you turn off the tap while you brush your teeth, you help the environment.

Caring for Nature

You can care for nature. You can care for plants.
You can care for animals.

When you do not pick **wild flowers**, you help the **environment**. When you do not touch bird nests or **wild animals**, you help the environment.

Caring for the Future

Caring for the **environment** will keep it clean and safe for the **future**.

We can care for the environment.

How Will You Care for the Environment Today?

 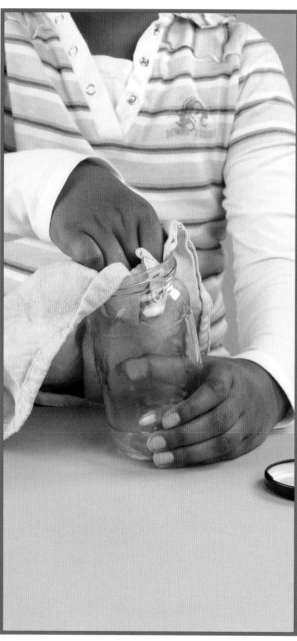 

Words to Know

air conditioners	machine used to cool the air indoors
energy	the power to move, change or grow. Things such as lights, computers, and cars need energy to make them work.
environment	the world around us
future	time that is going to come; What is going to happen. The future can refer to time minutes, days or even years ahead.
pollution	harmful dirt, waste gasses or chemicals. The air, water, or land can be polluted.
reuse	use again
recycle	make old things into new things
wild animals	animals that are not kept by people
wild flowers	flowers that grow naturally and are not planted or grown by people

Index

Note to Parents and Teachers

Before reading

Discuss with children about how the environment is the world around us. Plants and animals are a part of our environment. When people litter they harm our environment. Ask children what they know about litter? What ways can we protect our environment? Together, begin creating a KWL chart titled "Environment."
Write the following titles to create three columns: "What You Know," "What You Want to Know," " What You've Learned." Discuss the first two columns with the children and then fill the first two columns in.

After reading

Continue discussing and filling in the KWL chart with the children. Focus on the third column, "What You've Learned." Ask children what they learned from this book. After children have listed their ideas, discuss how they can protect our environment by picking up trash, recycling, turning off a faucet to conserve water, and only using lights when necessary. Have children create signs that show different ways to Help the Environment. If possible use recycled paper!